ᒧhristmas Extras: FAITH-FILLED IDEAS FOR CELEBRATING CHRISTMAS

oveland, Colorado

sit our Web site: **www.group.com**

REDITS
hief Creative Officer: Joani Schultz
hildren's Senior Developer: Patty Anderson
hildren's Ministry Champion: Christine Yount Jones
enior Editor: Jan Kershner
enior Art Director: Andrea Filer
lustrator/Designer: Patrick Creyts
roduction Manager: DeAnne Lear

BN 978-0-7644-3712-0
0 9 8 7 6 5 4 3 2 1   17 16 15 14 13 12 11 10 09 08
inted in the United States of America.

CONTENTS

ALLERGY ALERT

Each time you see the Allergy Alert symbol, take the necessary precautions. Be aware that some children have food allergies that can be dangerous. Know your children and consult with parents about allergies their children might have. Also be sure to read food labels carefully, as hidden ingredients can cause allergy-related problems.

Introduction

The Christmas season is a time of great excitement, especially for kids. It's a time of wonder, love, and anticipation!

Help your kids feel the excitement and anticipation of the amazing news the angel brought to Mary. You want them to model the obedience that Joseph showed when the angel brought him the same astonishing news. You want them to joyfully celebrate the miraculous birth of our Savior. And you want them to worship Jesus as the wise men did.

This little book can help! Use these easy, fun, faith-filled activities to help kids keep Jesus at the center of the Christmas season. Add these ideas to an existing lesson, or build a lesson of your own! Either way, you'll be filling kids with the faith they need to follow Jesus every day of their lives!

Get Ready for Jesus: Mary's Good News

BIBLE BASIS: Luke 1:26-38

For those who know Jesus, the preparation for Jesus' birthday brings deep feelings of wonder, joy, and love. The glorious birth of Jesus brings a message of promise to all those who hear and believe. It's that promise that Mary first rejoiced in, a promise that lasts for eternity.

Help children understand that the deep joy they can feel is not simply excitement for a coming holiday—it's their heartfelt connection to the promise that is Christ.

BIBLE EXPERIENCE

God Keeps His Promises

OBJECTIVE: Children will create backdrops that help them tell the story of the forecast of Jesus' birth.

SUPPLIES:

- Bibles
- newsprint
- safety scissors
- paper
- markers
- pencils

TIME: 20 to 25 minutes

PREPARATION: none

Form groups of three or four, and assign each group to read Luke 1:26-38. Give each group a large piece of newsprint, markers, and scissors.

In your group, take turns reading the verses from your Bible passage. Then use the markers to turn your paper into the background for a live mural of your story. Draw the background and bodies of the people involved in your story. Then cut out holes for the head and arms. The kids playing the characters in your story will put their heads and arms through the holes and act out the story for the rest of the class.

Provide paper and pencils for kids to create a script. Encourage them to use as much facial, arm, and hand motions in their script as possible. After several minutes, have groups display their live murals and present their dramas. Give each group a rousing round of applause.

- **What was the message the angel brought to Mary?**
- **Think of a time you were given very important news. Were you surprised? Did you believe the news?**

Ask a child to read aloud Luke 1:45.

- **What did Mary have to do to receive God's promise?**

Jesus' birth was the fulfillment of God's promises. The Bible tells us about Jesus, "All of God's promises have been fulfilled in Christ" (2 Corinthians 1:20). Let's repeat that verse together. Have kids repeat the verse with you.

When God promises something, we can believe it! God keeps his promises.

PRESCHOOL BIBLE EXPERIENCE

The Birth of Jesus Foretold

OBJECTIVE: Children will act out Mary's exciting visit from an angel.

SUPPLIES:

- Bible
- baby doll
- angel and Mary costumes (optional)

TIME: 10 to 15 minutes

PREPARATION: none

Have kids form a circle and sit down. Open your Bible to Luke 1, and show children the words. Choose two children to help you tell the story. Dress children in costumes if you have them.

In the town of Nazareth, there was a woman named Mary. Encourage "Mary" to stand up and wave at the group. Tell Mary to act out her part of the story as you speak. **One day Mary was in her house. Maybe she was looking out the window. Or maybe she was cleaning her floor. Or maybe she was washing her dishes. Then,**

all of a sudden, an angel appeared to Mary! Encourage "Gabriel" to stand up and wave at the group. Tell Gabriel to act out his part of the story as you speak.

The angel, Gabriel, said, "Greetings! The Lord is with you!" Encourage Gabriel to repeat the words after you. **Mary didn't know what to think. She shrugged her shoulders and wondered what the angel meant.**

"Don't worry, Mary," said Gabriel. Encourage Gabriel to repeat the words. **"God loves you, and he's going to give you a son."** Encourage Gabriel to repeat the words. **"Your son will be named Jesus, and he will be the Son of God."** Encourage Gabriel to repeat the words.

This really made Mary wonder. She shrugged her shoulders and shook her head. Then she asked Gabriel a question. "How can I have a baby? I'm not married!" Encourage Mary to repeat the words.

Gabriel smiled and told Mary not to worry. He told Mary that nothing was impossible with God and that God would give Mary the baby. **Mary smiled and smiled and smiled. She said to Gabriel, "I am the Lord's servant, and I will obey him."** Encourage Mary to repeat the words.

Re-enact the skit again using two different children. Repeat several times so all the kids get a chance to be in the skit.

Once you're finished acting out the story, have children stand in a circle. Choose a child to be the angel Gabriel, and have Gabriel hold a doll to represent baby Jesus. As the class sings "Mary Heard the Angel" to the tune of "The Mulberry Bush," have Gabriel walk around the inside of the circle, getting ready to choose a Mary. At the end of the song, have Gabriel hand the baby Jesus to the Mary of his or her choice. The child chosen then becomes the angel Gabriel.

Mary heard the angel say,
Angel say, angel say.
Mary heard the angel say
That Jesus would be born.

Jesus is God's only Son,
God's only Son, God's only Son.
Jesus is God's only Son.
His mother was Mary.

A long time before Mary was alive, God told the people that he would send his Son to earth to save everyone. God kept his promise and sent Jesus to earth as the son of Mary. God keeps his promises!

- **How has God kept his promises to you?**
- **How can you thank God for keeping his promises?**

SCIENCE DEVOTION

The Power of God's Promises

OBJECTIVE: Children will compare the strength of reinforced cardboard to the strength our faith can have when it's reinforced with prayer.

SUPPLIES:
- Bible
- two 4x12-inch strips of corrugated cardboard
- one 12-ounce frozen juice can
- masking tape or rubber bands
- 2 heavy books

TIME: 10 to 15 minutes

PREPARATION: none

- **Can you think of any people today who aren't sure they believe God's promises?**

This experiment will help us see that God's promises make us strong. Have a child help you wrap a piece of cardboard around the juice can, and let another child wrap masking tape around the cardboard to keep it firmly in place. Slide the juice can out of the cardboard.

•What are some of God's promises?
•How do these promises keep you strong?
•How strong do you think this cardboard is? Do you think it's strong enough for a book to sit on?

Give one volunteer a heavy book and the piece of flat cardboard.

Try to hold up your piece of cardboard on one edge on the table (or the floor), and then try to balance the book on top. Give the child a few seconds to do this.

Give a second volunteer the cardboard tube and the other heavy book.

I'd like you to try to balance the book on top of the cardboard tube.

•Which is stronger: the cardboard piece or the tube? Why?

Cardboard is a strong material. But cardboard is even stronger when we form it in a different shape and reinforce it with masking tape (or rubber bands), as we did with this tube.

• How is this like God's Word and promises?

Read aloud 2 Corinthians 1:20.

The promises of God are strong. And the strongest promise he ever gave us was his Son, Jesus.

•What can you do to shape your life so your life will thank God for his greatest promise to you?

GAME

Mystery Bag

OBJECTIVE: By asking questions, children will determine the contents of a "Mystery Bag," then talk about getting ready for Christmas.

SUPPLIES:

- 1 paper bag
- 1 string of Christmas lights
- 1 Christmas tree ornament
- 1 bow
- 1 candy cane

TIME: 10 minutes

PREPARATION: Before children arrive put all the items into the paper bag.

Explain that you have a mystery bag filled with things used to get ready for Christmas. Mentally choose one item from the bag to use first.

Have children take turns asking yes and no questions to determine the item. It they haven't guessed after 10 questions, reveal the item.

Play again, using the other items in the bag.

- **How do these objects get us ready for Christmas?**
- **Are there any objects that could help us get ready for Jesus? If so, what are they?**

No matter what time of year it is, we can get ready for Jesus.

CRAFT

Good News Garland

OBJECTIVE: Kids can spread the good news of Christmas to their neighbors with this simple craft.

SUPPLIES:
- plastic cling wrap
- red and green ribbon
- Christmas invitation
- hard Christmas candy

TIME: 20 to 25 minutes

PREPARATION: none

Give each child 2 feet of plastic cling wrap. Place candies in a line lengthwise on the cling wrap about 1 inch apart. Carefully roll the cling wrap around the candies to create a 2-foot candy rope. Tie ribbons on both ends of the rope and between each piece of candy. Kids can share their favorite things about Christmas for each tie. Attach an invitation card to the garland that includes the time, date, and location of your Christmas Eve service.

Have kids imagine and describe what it would be like to celebrate Christmas without knowing about Jesus.

Christmas is a great time to invite your neighbors and friends to church. Use this Good News Garland to extend an invitation to our Christmas Eve service.

Angel Announcements: An Angel Appears to Joseph

BIBLE BASIS: Matthew 1:18-23
God sent an angel to Joseph to announce the promise of his Son. Oh, the questions that must have entered Joseph's and Mary's minds: *How can this be? Why us? What will people say?* Scripture tells us that Joseph and Mary believed the angel's promise, humbly trusting God's will for their lives.

You can help instill that same trust in young children. They can trust God's plans through his Word, through others, and through prayer. Use this lesson to encourage your students to trust in God and rely on his plans.

BIBLE EXPERIENCE

Trust God's Plans

OBJECTIVE: Children will create new names that reflect ways to serve God.

SUPPLIES:
- Bible
- markers
- index cards
- tape

TIME: 15 to 20 minutes

PREPARATION: If you like, bring in a book of names and their meanings so all the children can find the meanings of their names.

Have children form trios, and hand everyone a card and a marker.

All of us have names that we're known by. Most of our names have certain meanings. Allow children who know the meanings of their names to share them with the class.

Read aloud Matthew 1:1-17.

That's a lot of names! This history of Jesus' family tells us how Jesus descended from Abraham and David, just as God told the prophets.

Did you know that Jesus has other names besides Jesus? Listen for one of Jesus' other names while I read. When you hear it, put your hand over your heart.

Read aloud Matthew 1:18-23. Pause, and then read verse 23 again, asking children to repeat it with you.

- **What does *Immanuel* mean?**
- **How did Jesus fulfill the meaning of that name, "God is with us"?**
- **What's so important about having God present with us?**

Jesus also has names that tell more about him. Some are "Bread of Life," "Good Shepherd," and "the Way and the Truth." All of his names remind us of the different ways Jesus works in God's plans.

Read Matthew 1:24-25.

After Joseph realized what God told him, he changed his plans to divorce Mary. By taking on the role of Mary's husband and Jesus' father, Joseph chose to trust God's plans and to serve God. Think of ways you can trust and serve God. Then create a new name for yourself that describes a way you can serve God. On your card, write your new name and the way you can serve God. For example, if I want to serve God by singing, then my new name could be *Songster* or *Tuneful*.

Allow children several minutes to create their new names. Allow them to tape the index cards to themselves and wear the cards as name tags.

Joseph trusted God, risking his reputation and professional life, because he knew God's plans were more important. We can trust God's plans, too.

PRESCHOOL BIBLE EXPERIENCE

An Angel Appears to Joseph

OBJECTIVE: Children will create puppets and discover that they can trust God's plans.

SUPPLIES:
- Bible
- brown paper lunch bags
- craft sticks
- aluminum foil
- glue
- construction paper
- glitter
- markers
- white crayons

TIME: 15 to 20 minutes

PREPARATION: Set out the craft supplies.

Have kids form a circle and sit down. Give each child three brown paper bags and one small craft stick. Encourage kids to use foil, glitter, and white crayons to decorate one brown paper sack as an angel puppet. Tell kids to use the markers and construction paper to decorate one of the other puppets as Joseph and the other puppet as Mary. Have kids draw a baby on the craft stick. Tell kids to use their puppets to act out the story as you tell it.

Open your Bible to Matthew 1, and show children the words.

Joseph was planning to be married to Mary. But when Joseph found out that she was going to have a baby, he was a little worried. Encourage children to make their Joseph puppets shake their heads and mumble. **Joseph didn't know that Mary was going to have God's Son!**

One night Joseph was asleep. Encourage children to make their Joseph puppets sleep. **While he was sleeping, he had a dream. An angel appeared to him in his dream.** Encourage kids to bring out their angel puppets. **The angel said to Joseph, "Don't be afraid to marry Mary. She loves God, and the baby she will have is God's Son!"** Let children use their angel puppets to repeat the angel's words, "You should name the baby Jesus because the baby will grow up to save the world." Encourage kids to have their angel puppets repeat those words. **Then the angel disappeared and Joseph woke up.** Encourage children to have their Joseph puppets wake up.

Joseph believed what the angel said, and he chose to trust God's plans. He married Mary, and when her son was born, they named him Jesus.

Encourage children to bring out their Mary puppets and pretend to have Mary and Joseph get married. Then have kids glue the small craft stick "baby Jesus" to their Mary puppets.

When you're finished with the story, have kids sing the following song to the tune of "London Bridge." Choose two kids to be the bridge, and encourage the other kids to walk under the "bridge." At the end of the song, the bridge should collapse and capture one child.

Joseph, you can trust God's plans,
Trust God's plans, trust God's plans.
Joseph, you can trust God's plans
Because God loves you!

When kids capture a student in their arms, tell them to sing the song again, using the captured child's name in place of Joseph's name. Then let the captured child choose another child, and those two children will become the new bridge. Continue playing until each child gets a chance to be captured and play the bridge.

Remind children that they can always trust God's plans.

- **How did Joseph trust God's plans?**
- **How can you trust God's plans for your life?**

SNACK

Heavenly Wedding Cake

OBJECTIVE: Children will create tiny wedding cakes to remind them how God told Joseph that he should still take Mary as his wife.

SUPPLIES:

ALLERGY ALERT

- 3 vanilla wafers per child
- 2 tablespoons white frosting per child
- 2 gummi bears per child
- plastic knives or craft sticks for spreading
- paper plates
- baby wipes

TIME: 15 to 20 minutes

PREPARATION: Set out your snack supplies.

Today we're learning that God has good plans for us, even if we don't understand those plans. Joseph didn't understand the plans God had for him, but he trusted God and obeyed.

Joseph thought that he should call off his marriage when he found out that Mary was going to have a baby. But an angel from God told Joseph in a dream to go ahead with the wedding. Let's make a wedding cake to celebrate Mary and Joseph's marriage!

Have children clean their hands thoroughly both before and after making snacks.

Have each child spread some frosting onto one of his or her vanilla wafers. Show children how to create two more layers on top of their cookies by alternating icing and cookies.

After the third wafer has been placed on top, have children cover the entire cookie stack with white icing, creating a mini "cake."

Have kids place two gummi bears on top of their "wedding cakes" as the bride and groom figures.

Let's enjoy our snacks.

- **Have you ever been to a wedding? If so, what was it like?**

ASK:
- How do you think Joseph felt when God sent the angel?
- How do you feel knowing God has good plans for you?

Joseph trusted God's good plans for his life, and so can we!

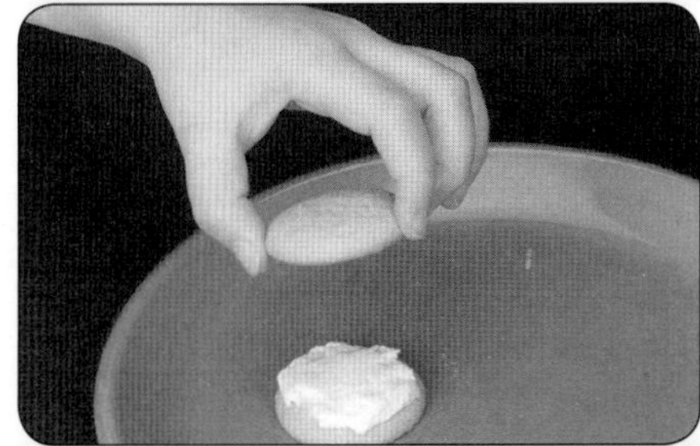

Tip

For added fun perform a mini wedding ceremony using your gummi bears! Children can hum wedding music and march their bears "down the aisle" and onto the tops of their cakes.

OBJECT LESSON

Strength in His Plans

OBJECTIVE: Children will see how God's plans can strengthen them.

SUPPLIES:
- Bible
- small polished stones

TIME: 5 to 10 minutes

PREPARATION: Conceal a stone in one hand before you begin to speak. You'll need one small stone for each child.

Hold out both fists.

I have something in one of my hands. Can you guess which one? Let kids guess. Try this a few times, each time putting your hands behind your back to conceal where the stone is.

Hold out the stone in one hand for kids to see.

God never makes us try to guess the wrong answer. Read aloud Matthew 1:23. **He told the prophets that a Savior was coming, and he did! When we trust in God's plans, we strengthen our faith in him. It will be as strong as this rock!**

Give each child a polished stone.

Trust in God's plans, and he will be with you always. Hold your shiny stone firmly in your hand as we thank God for his rock-solid promise—his Son, Jesus. Close in a prayer of thanks for the birth of the Savior.

CREATIVE PRAYER

Prayer Chain

OBJECTIVE: Children will make visual reminders of their answered prayers.

SUPPLIES:

- scissors
- transparent tape
- construction paper (2 colors)
- fine-point markers or pens

TIME: 10 to 15 minutes

PREPARATION: Use scissors to create a supply of 1x6-inch construction paper strips of two colors. Set out the strips, along with the fine-point markers or pens, and the transparent tape. Designate one color of paper strips for prayer requests and the other for answered prayers.

Encourage each child to write a prayer request or a brief description of an answered prayer on a paper strip of the appropriate color. Then have kids loop and tape the paper slips together (with the writing on the outside) to make a prayer chain. Tell kids that colors don't have to alternate in this paper chain. Hang the chain from a corner of your ceiling.

Allow time for kids to add to the prayer chain. As they work, ask them to offer what's on their chain link silently to God and then close by saying aloud, "I trust in God's plans." As the chain grows, hang it festively around the room.

Jesus Is Born!

BIBLE BASIS: Luke 2:1-20
God entrusted an amazing message to humble, ordinary people—shepherds. They were the ones trumpeting the message in the streets of Bethlehem: The Messiah is born!

Teach children that this message of hope and joy isn't just for an elite few. The shepherds told everyone—they were passionate about the message. We can be, too!

BIBLE EXPERIENCE

God Sent Us a Savior

OBJECTIVE: Children will make a crystal painting of the Nativity.

SUPPLIES:
- Bible
- dark-colored construction paper
- small paintbrushes
- cups
- water
- teaspoon
- salt

TIME: 10 to 15 minutes

PREPARATION: You'll need access to an oven.

Read aloud Luke 2:1-20. Then give each child a sheet of paper, a paintbrush, and a cup of water with 3 teaspoons of salt. Have children create a Christmas scene telling the news of Jesus' birth. Tell children to dip and stir with the brush before writing each letter or drawing each image.

As children work, preheat the oven to 150 degrees. Repeat Luke 2:11 several times to remind children of the wonderful good news they're announcing: "The Savior—yes, the Messiah, the Lord—has been born today in Bethlehem." Bake the finished scenes for five minutes or until the papers dry. The images will appear as sparkling crystals on the dark paper.

After the pictures are finished, set them aside.

ASK:

- **Were you surprised at how your amazing messages turned out? Explain.**
- **How do you think the shepherds felt when they saw the angels?**
- **If you had been with the shepherds, how would you have reacted?**

The angels brought wonderful news: God sent us a Savior. Although the shepherds were surprised at the message, they went to Bethlehem and found Jesus, just as the angels had said. Everyone who heard the news was amazed.

We can also share the amazing news that God sent us a Savior. Take home your amazing message, and give it to someone you'd like to tell about Jesus.

PRESCHOOL BIBLE EXPERIENCE

The Birth of Jesus

OBJECTIVE: Children will participate in an active telling of the Christmas story.

SUPPLIES:

- Bible
- large bells for each child

TIME: 15 to 20 minutes

PREPARATION: none

Have kids form a circle and sit down. Open your Bible to Luke 2, and show children the words.

Today's Bible story comes from the book of Luke. There are many angels in this story. An angel is a special messenger from God. Every time you hear me say *angel*, I want you to shout out, "Praise God!"

When Mary was about to have her baby, Mary and Joseph had to go on a long trip back to the town where Joseph was born. When it

was time for God to give baby Jesus to Mary and Joseph, they had to find a place to stay for the night. But no one had a room. The only place for Mary to rest was in a stable where farm animals lived—in a barn.

- **Can you name an animal that lives in a barn?**
- **What sound does that animal make?**

These are some of the animals and sounds that might have filled the place where Jesus was born. Mary wrapped baby Jesus in cloth to keep him warm and laid him in a manger to sleep. Have the children pretend to wrap a blanket around a baby and rock it back and forth.

Meanwhile, shepherds were taking care of their sheep in the fields. Encourage children to make sheep sounds. **It was late at night when angels** (have children shout, "Praise God!") **appeared to the shepherds. The whole sky was filled with angels.** Have children shout, "Praise God!" **They told the shepherds that baby Jesus was born and that he would take away the bad things people did. The angels** (have children shout, "Praise God!") **told the shepherds that they could find baby Jesus in the city of Bethlehem. So the shepherds ran to find Jesus—the baby King that God had promised for so many years to send.**

When the shepherds saw baby Jesus, they were very happy! They told everyone what the angels (have children shout, "Praise God!") **had said. "Jesus came to take away our sins," they said. The shepherds were very happy that Jesus was born to save everyone.**

Give children bells to shake while they sing "Jesus Came" to the tune of "Jingle Bells."

Jesus came.
Jesus came.
Jesus came to show
That he's God's Son and he's the one
God promised long ago.
(Repeat.)

- **Why was Jesus born?**
- **How can you thank Jesus for coming to save us?**

GAME

Bethlehem Balloons

OBJECTIVE: Children will take a census of balloons.

SUPPLIES:

- Bible
- balloons

TIME: 5 to 10 minutes

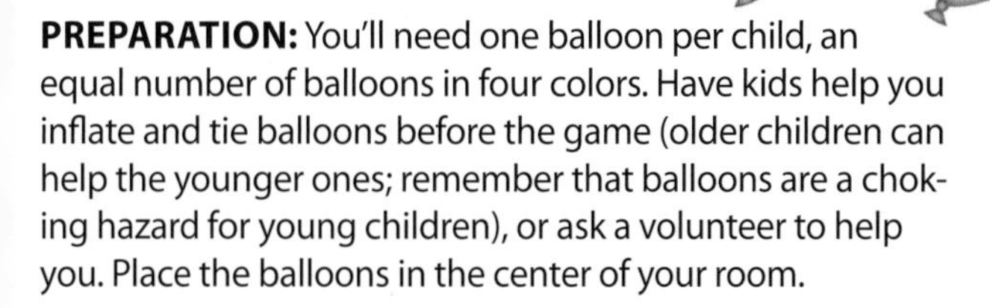

PREPARATION: You'll need one balloon per child, an equal number of balloons in four colors. Have kids help you inflate and tie balloons before the game (older children can help the younger ones; remember that balloons are a choking hazard for young children), or ask a volunteer to help you. Place the balloons in the center of your room.

Give each child a balloon. Ask kids to scatter around the room so they're equally spaced throughout your playing area, and have them sit down.

Read aloud Luke 2:1-5.

Joseph had to take Mary to his hometown to be counted in a census. It's time to take a census of the balloons. All our balloons must be counted, and to be counted they must return to their "hometowns." Designate the corners of your playing area as the hometowns. Assign one color to each corner.

There's one catch with the balloon census: You have to bat the balloons to the correct corners without standing up or moving.

Tell kids to begin, and then stand back and watch the fun! When all the balloons have been batted to the corners, close the game by asking each child to go to a corner, find one balloon, and sit on it to break it. As each child breaks a balloon, help him or her count out "one," "two," and so on until kids have counted all the balloons in each corner. At the end of the game, discuss the following questions:

- **How easy or hard was it for you to get your balloon to its corner?**
- **How is that like how Joseph and Mary might have felt when they had to go to Bethlehem to be counted in a census?**
- **How do you think they felt knowing that God was sending a Savior?**

Read aloud the rest of the story from Luke 2:6-20.

SNACK

Shepherd's Speedy Goodies

OBJECTIVE: Children will make easy-to-carry snacks to remind them of the shepherds who hurried off to find Jesus.

SUPPLIES:

ALLERGY ALERT

- 1 plastic resealable sandwich bag per child
- 2 tablespoons chocolate chips per child
- 2 tablespoons raisins per child
- 2 tablespoons Cheerios per child
- bowls
- measuring spoons
- baby wipes

TIME: 15 to 20 minutes

PREPARATION: Before children arrive, put the snack ingredients into bowls. If you have a large group of children, make extra bowls so children will have easier access to the ingredients.

An angel appeared to a group of shepherds and told them that a Savior had been born! When the shepherds heard the good news, they hurried off to find this baby.

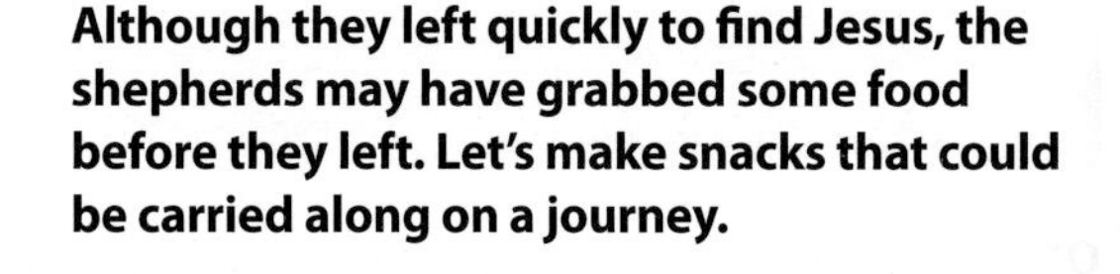

Although they left quickly to find Jesus, the shepherds may have grabbed some food before they left. Let's make snacks that could be carried along on a journey.

Have children clean their hands thoroughly both before and after making snacks.

Have each child scoop two tablespoons each of the chocolate chips, raisins, and Cheerios into his or her plastic bag.

Let's enjoy our snacks.

- **How would you feel if angels suddenly appeared before you?**
- **What are ways that Jesus helps you and your family?**
- **What are ways you can help your family this week?**

Tip

You can also substitute other trail mix items such as marshmallows, other types of dry cereals, or small crackers for the items in this snack.

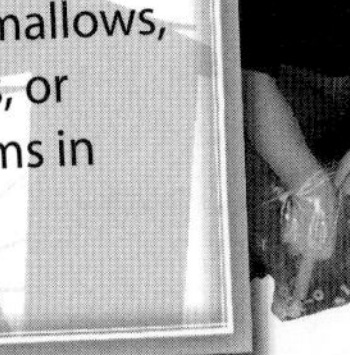

CELEBRATION EVENT

Mega Birthday Bash

OBJECTIVE: Children will enjoy a fun birthday party for Jesus.

SUPPLIES:

- party invitations
- balloons
- party decorations
- decorated cupcakes
- candles
- craft supplies

ALLERGY ALERT

TIME: 1 hour

PREPARATION: Two weeks prior to the event, send birthday party invitations to kids to announce the birthday bash and encourage them to bring their friends and neighbors.

Before the day of the party, decorate and set up the booths as described in the activity.

Sponsor a huge birthday bash at your church to celebrate Jesus' birth.

For the birthday bash, create booths with party games such as Pin the Gift on the Wise Man, Christmas Musical Chairs, and Christmas Star Twister. Include face painting and a cupcake stand where kids receive a cupcake with a birthday candle they can blow out. Stock another booth with paper, markers, decorative scissors, glitter, glue, and stickers to make Christmas cards for people in a nursing home or at a shelter.

Decorate with streamers, balloons, and banners. Play kids' favorite Christmas carols. Give kids birthday hats and party bags to collect candy from each booth. For extra fun, recruit clowns and balloon artists to wander through the party as they share the story of Jesus' birth and the amazing gift God has given us.

CREATIVE PRAYER

Crèche Prayer

OBJECTIVE: Children will set up a crèche as they pray.

SUPPLIES:
- crèche scene
- box
- wrapping paper

TIME: 5 to 10 minutes

PREPARATION: Pack the figures from a crèche scene in a box.

Allow kids to take turns unwrapping figures. As they add the figures to the crèche scene, have them give thanks for the role that figure played in Jesus' birth. For instance, the person holding the stable might say, "Thank you that there was at least a stable nearby for Jesus." The person with a shepherd might say, "Thank you that the shepherds went and told lots of people about Jesus."

After all the kids have added their figures and prayed, close with a group prayer, asking God to help everyone remember that Jesus is our Savior.

CRAFT

Angelic Announcement Ornament

OBJECTIVE: Children will make an angel ornament as a reminder of the angels that announced the birth of Christ.

SUPPLIES:
- one 1-inch wooden bead per child
- one 1½-inch tall clay pot per child
- one 13-mm jingle bell per child
- one chenille wire per child
- stickers
- markers
- glitter
- 2 disposable plates
- glue

TIME: 20 to 25 minutes

PREPARATION: Set out plates of glue.

Tip

Before children arrive, pour glue and glitter onto disposable plates, preparing one of each for every four or five kids. For faster drying, use tacky glue.

When Jesus was born, angels told shepherds that Jesus had come. Let's make angel ornaments to remind us that Jesus is born.

Show children how to thread their chenille wires through their jingle bells. Have children put the wires through the holes in the pots so the bells are inside the pots, then thread the wires through the wooden beads. Have kids twist the wires to make a loop at the top.

The wooden bead will be the angel's head. Let children draw faces on their angels, then attach their stickers to the clay pot.

Show children how to dip the bottom of their angels into the plate of glue then into the plate of glitter to make a rim of glitter.

- **What do you think it was like for the shepherds to see the angels?**
- **How can you use your ornament to tell someone that Jesus is born?**
- **What are ways that you can tell others that Jesus is born?**

Wise Men Worship Jesus

BIBLE BASIS: Matthew 2:1-12
The Magi followed the star to Bethlehem, where their predictions about a new king were confirmed. They worshipped Jesus joyfully, and presented him with precious gifts.

Children love to give and receive gifts during the Christmas season. Use these activities to help your kids realize that they can give Jesus good gifts, too.

BIBLE EXPERIENCE FOR ALL AGES

Wise Men Worship

OBJECTIVE: Children love to give and receive gifts at Christmastime. As you teach this lesson, you will help kids see that they can give Jesus good gifts also.

SUPPLIES:
- Bible
- 1-foot-long piece of aluminum foil for each child
- doll

TIME: 10 minutes

PREPARATION: Before you begin, mold a 1-foot-long piece of aluminum foil into the shape of a star.

Gather the class around you in a circle on the floor. Open your Bible to the book of Matthew, and show it to children.

Today's Bible adventure is from the book of Matthew. In a country far away from where Jesus was born, there lived some wise men. The wise men had been watching a special star in the sky. Hold the foil over your head. **The wise men knew that God put this star in the sky to tell them that Jesus, the promised King, was born. They knew that if they followed the star, it would lead them to where the promised King would be.**

But first they wanted to prepare special gifts to give to Jesus. Let's pretend to make gifts

for Jesus by shaping these pieces of foil into whatever you want.

Give each child a piece of aluminum foil. Instruct kids to mold their foil into the shapes of gifts that they would have liked to give Jesus.

The wise men prepared gifts of gold and nice-smelling perfumes and spices. Then they followed the star. Hold up the star over your head, and lead the children to the opposite side of the room—around tables, chairs, and toys. Have a doll sitting in your dramatic play area, and tell the children to pretend it's little Jesus.

When they found Jesus, they gave him their gifts. Have children set their foil gifts on the ground in front of the doll. **They worshipped Jesus. They were so happy that God helped them meet Jesus, the promised King.**

- **What do you think you might say to Jesus?**
- **If you were a wise man, what kind of gift would you give to Jesus?**

We may not be rich or extra-smart like the wise men, but we can give special gifts to Jesus, too.

GAME

Stargazers

OBJECTIVE: Children will search for a glow-in-the-dark star as a reminder of the Magi searching for Jesus.

SUPPLIES:
- 1 small plastic glow-in-the dark star per child, plus 1 extra star

TIME: 10 minutes

PREPARATION: none

Hold one star up to the light to "charge" it and make it glow brightly.

Have the children shut their eyes. Silently give one child the star, then let everyone open their eyes.

Turn off the lights and let children quietly move around the room. After a few seconds, ask the child with the star to hold it where others can see it if they're looking.

When children see the glowing star they should stand beside the child holding it until everyone has found the star. Play again as time allows.

- **What made finding the star difficult?**
- **How can this game remind us of the wise men searching for Jesus?**

The Magi followed the star to find Jesus. We can find Jesus without traveling anywhere. One of the easiest ways to find Jesus is by reading the Bible. Each of you can take a star home to put in a dark place as a reminder to look for Jesus each day.

Give each child a glow-in-the-dark star.

SNACK

Magi Mix-Up

OBJECTIVE: Children will create an edible gift and then, with the gift and a partner, play the Magi Mix-Up game.

SUPPLIES:
- 1 two-inch cube of Rice Krispie treat per child
- 1 foot-long piece of thin licorice per child
- 3 paper cups per pair (cups must be 9 ounces or larger)
- 3 napkins per child
- baby wipes

ALLERGY ALERT

TIME: 15 to 20 minutes

PREPARATION: none

SAY: **The Magi were wise men who wanted to find Jesus. King Herod told them to find Jesus and then come back and tell him where Jesus was. But God let the Magi know that Herod only wanted to harm Jesus, so they gave Herod the mix-up! Instead of going back to Herod, the wise men went home a different way.**

Today, you'll hide and find a gift to remind you of the Magi's clever actions, but also to remind you that Jesus is God's gift to us and that we can find Jesus wherever we are!

Have children clean their hands thoroughly both before and after making snacks.

Have each child use a piece of licorice to tie a bow onto a small cube of Rice Krispie treat. Encourage older children to assist younger ones with this task.

Have children form pairs. Demonstrate how they can take turns hiding the Krispie-treat present under a paper cup and on top of a napkin for one another in a guessing game.

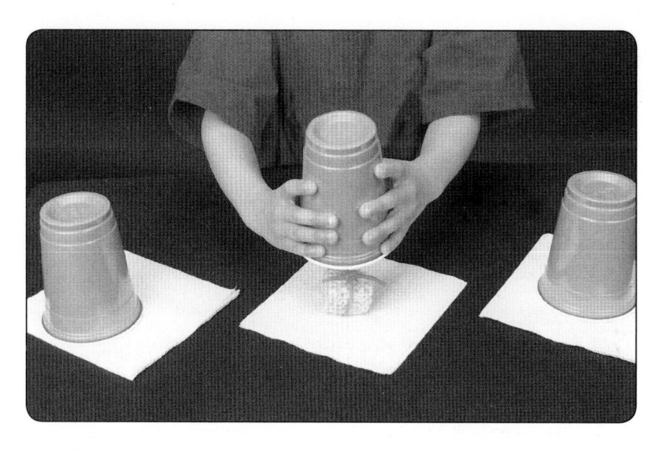

Let the child hiding the present shuffle around the hidden gift with two other upside-down cups. Have the partner guess which cup the gift is under. Ask partners to switch roles, then let them eat their snacks.

Have kids eat their snacks.

- **Have you ever found a hidden gift or something you thought was a treasure? If so, how did it feel?**
- **How do you think the Magi felt finding Jesus?**
- **How can we find Jesus today?**

CRAFT

Three Gifts and a Star

OBJECTIVE: Children will create wave bottles to symbolize the gifts the Magi brought to Jesus.

SUPPLIES:

- 1 clean, clear plastic 16-ounce bottle with lid per child
- food coloring
- 1/2 cup vegetable oil per child
- 1/2 teaspoon gold glitter per child
- 1 gold foil confetti star per child
- water
- funnels
- glue

TIME: 10 to 15 minutes

PREPARATION: none

Magi, or wise men, followed a star to find Jesus. They brought Jesus gifts of gold, frankincense, and myrrh. We all know what gold is, but you may not know that frankincense is an oil that smells like strong perfume. Myrrh is another oil that is used in medicines. Both of these were very valuable in Bible times. Our project today will remind us of the gifts the Magi brought to Jesus, and that just like the Magi, we can find Jesus.

Have children pour 1/2 teaspoon of glitter into their bottles, then use a funnel to add 1/2 cup of vegetable oil. Tell kids this represents the gifts of gold and myrrh.

Let children fill their bottles almost to the rim with water and add a few drops of any color of food coloring. This will represent the frankincense.

Let each child drop one gold foil confetti star into his or her bottle to represent the star the Magi followed. Have kids spread glue around the top outer edge of their bottles, then securely tighten the lids over the glue.

Show children how to gently shake the bottles to mix the contents, then watch the contents swirl and separate. See if children can find the star as it mixes with the glitter.

- **How can you use this wave bottle to tell others the story of the Magi?**
- **What gifts do you think Jesus would like you to give him?**
- **How can we find Jesus today?**

Tip

Twenty-four or 20-ounce water bottles can also be used for this project. Simply add more water, leaving other amounts the same.

BIBLE APPLICATION

Where's Jesus?

OBJECTIVE: Children will draw an invisible picture of Jesus and then make it appear.

SUPPLIES:

- 1 small bowl of lemon juice for every four or five kids
- 1 sheet of white paper per child
- 1 cotton swab per child
- sheets of newspaper
- 1 iron
- Christmas carol CD
- CD player

TIME: 25 to 30 minutes

PREPARATION: Prepare the bowls of lemon juice.

The Magi, or wise men, knew from their studies that the Messiah was coming. The Magi followed God's signs and found Jesus. Let's do an experiment to help us think about how we can find Jesus.

Have children use cotton swabs dipped in the lemon juice to draw a picture of baby Jesus. The lemon juice acts as invisible ink, so the children won't be able to see their work clearly.

After the children have made their pictures, allow them to dry for a few minutes. Sing one of the kids' favorite Christmas songs while the pictures dry.

Iron over children's papers one at a time to make the pictures appear. Place several sheets of newspaper on tables before ironing.

- **What surprised you about this project?**
- **What helped the Magi find Jesus?**
- **How can we find Jesus today?**

Tip

Be sure only adults use the hot irons. Remind children to allow their pictures to cool for several seconds before touching them after they're ironed.